# Card Tricks

This is a Parragon Book
This edition published in 2004

Parragon
Queen Street House
4 Queen Street
Bath BA1 1HE, UK

ISBN: 1-40543-908-4

A copy of the CIP data for this book is available from the British
Library upon request.

The right of Louis Canasta to be identified as the author of this work
has been asserted in accordance with Section 77 of the Copyright,
Designs and Patents Act of 1988.

Printed and bound in China

# Card Tricks

## Louis Canasta

# Contents

It Must be Magic   5

  Getting Going   9

  Preparation   10

  Practise   12

  Patter   13

  Presentation   14

Pick a Card ... any Card   18

  The Glimpse   18

  Shuffling – Genuinely or Otherwise   20

  Rise and Fall   24

  The False Cut   25

And for my Next Trick...   28

  Good Vibrations   29

  Counting Off   30

  Under or Over   33

  Talk to the Queen   34

  Have You Seen It Yet?   36

  The Clock Never Lies   38

  Copping Off   40

  The Piano Player   41

  The Sandwich   44

  You Do It, Then!   46

# It Must be Magic

Everybody loves a magician. If you can stand in front of people and perform a trick that confounds their logic then you'll be the most popular person in that room, as to do magic is guaranteed to impress people to a far greater degree than if you can sing, dance or wrestle alligators. Also, it's much less likely to attract a police presence if you want to do it in public or on your mum's living-room carpet.

The best thing about doing magic is that nobody over the age of eight or nine *really* believes in it, but everybody *wants* to. You don't have to convince your audience that you've actually read their mind or made a card move up or down an unattended deck, you just have to amaze them with your skill and keep them entertained while you're doing it. The whole point is they will try their hardest to figure out how a trick was done, but end up being baffled by what they can come up with. Then provided they had a good time while they were being bamboozled – i.e. you made them chuckle, got them involved and generally put on a show – they'll be gagging for more. Buy a bigger letter box, as the sheer volume of party invitations will clog up the one you've got now.

And card tricks are probably the most effective magic you can perform. Not by any means the simplest, or the least impressive, but in practical terms. With most card tricks there are no complicated props, no big stages and nothing involving livestock, ladies or electric saws. Card tricks can be done any time anywhere, and to perform the tricks in *Card Tricks* – with the exception of one – all you'll need is a pack of cards, maybe a table, quick hands, amusing patter and an audience. In most cases when you perform card tricks you can astonish folk in the space you stand up in, adding a certain casualness of approach which, in turn, enormously increases your impressiveness factor.

However, don't think this means card tricks should be approached casually. Nearly every card trick known to man relies on one or more of the few basic techniques that will allow you to find a card that has been inserted at random into the pack, to reveal what card an audience member has picked or to predict what the top or bottom card is in a shuffled deck. All prospective magicians have to master these procedures before they can begin performing, thus *Card Tricks* is laid out to explain these first, before breaking down the tricks themselves into sections that use different techniques as their basis.

As a 'beginners' book', the tricks contained in *Card Tricks* are among the easiest to master and particularly appropriate for the younger magician. The book won't turn you into David Blaine overnight – in fact it won't turn you into anything overnight other than a few hours older – but it will let you in on a few trade secrets and introduce you to what fun this sort of magic can be. By providing a basis for the understanding and performance of elementary card tricks, and thus a grounding in doing magic in general, *Card Tricks* aims to get you started on the road to Blaineship rather than teaching you a few tricks as an end in itself.

There is no complicated sleight of hand within these pages, as not to get that sort of thing exactly right will give the whole game away; and none of these tricks involves pre-arranged packs, as I'm sure you've got more exciting things to do at the moment than remember how to remember the order of 52 cards plus jokers. Not that this in any way diminishes their effect, it merely provides a logical starting point and will allow you to wow your friends and family that bit sooner. Which has to be a good thing.

The best way to approach *Card Tricks* is first to read it all the way through, then return to the Pick a Card ... any Card section and start to teach yourself the techniques. Master these one at a time, then begin to incorporate them into tricks and start constructing your act complete with all the flourishes and patter that will turn it into a performance. And don't forget the magician's golden rule – you should be having fun. Performing card tricks is all about entertainment, and if you're not enjoying yourself then how can you expect your audience to?

So what are you waiting for? Grab a pack of cards and let's get set to astonish.

## Getting Going

There is one simple rule that all good magicians abide by. It is known as 'The Four Ps Rule' and it goes like this: Practise, practise, practise. And when you've finished practising, practise some more. While, once you've mastered a repertoire of tricks, this rule will never let you down, there is another set of guidelines that is equally useful for those starting out, and I call this 'The Other Four Ps Rule': Preparation,

Practise, Patter and Presentation. All four of these Ps are vital if you want to make the impact your card magic deserves, so let's look at them individually.

## Preparation

Apart from learning a trick and making sure you have everything you need in place, there are other crucial aspects of preparation.

1) Make sure the cards 'work'. That is, they can be manipulated smoothly and quickly. Brand-new cards will often stick to each other and require too much finger force, which means you'll have less control over what they do. Very old cards on the other hand don't stack together too well as the edges have roughened up and they are starting to crinkle. A broken-in deck will be ideal, one that has been used for a while but isn't starting to wear out.

2) Warm up before you get in front of your audience. Deal a few hands, go through some trick shuffles and cuts, generally mess about with a deck of cards just to get any stiffness out of your fingers and to put your head in that card trick place.

3) Get a trick right in your mind. Reach a point at which you are sure you are so comfortable with every step of it that you don't have to think about it consciously while you do it.

4) Never go in front of an audience with a trick you haven't 'road-tested' privately on somebody who will look for faults or inherent sloppiness.

5) Listen to them!

6) Learn a few tricks properly instead of a lot of tricks badly.

## Practise

Although I told you earlier that you can't do too much of this, there are some guidelines that ought to be applied.

1) Practise in a lot of short sessions rather than one or two long ones. This is because you'll grasp things so much better when you are fresh and it removes the likelihood of frustration having a serious negative effect – if something refuses to go right then pack up and come back to it at another time.

2) Practise one trick at a time. Saves a great deal of confusion!

3) Don't be afraid to rewrite the book. *Card Tricks* isn't written on tablets of stone, it's an explanation of each trick's basics – what I'll be teaching you is the way in which they work best for me, and that might not be how they work best for you. Any manual awkwardness will show up and detract from your

performance, so if your fingers are more comfortable doing something in a slightly different way, feel free to make the necessary adjustments.

4) Once you think you've mastered a trick, practise it in front of a mirror – full length if you've got one – for two excellent reasons. You can practise making eye contact with yourself and keep from looking down at your hands (see PRESENTATION), then if you check what you are actually doing through the mirror it will give a pretty accurate idea of what your audience will be able to see.

## Patter

Every magician needs good patter, and the emphasis here is on the 'good'. As I've said, you're there to entertain as much as to amaze, so tell stories, crack jokes, ask questions and encourage audience involvement. Develop a stage character that appears natural and relaxed and you can keep up without it flagging – comedy voices are not advised. As well as the putting on a show factor, slick patter and a good rapport will relax both you and your audience, which will allow you to gain their trust so they won't be overly suspicious of what it is you're actually doing. Critically, though, it will help you direct their attention anywhere you want to, which usually will be well away from what you're actually doing. Your patter – both style and content – is something else that should be thoroughly road-tested before you try it out in public.

A WORD OF WARNING: Try to avoid the words 'And for my next trick ...' or 'Pick a card ... any card' as the chances are you'll sound like an idiot.

## Presentation

As much as your vocal delivery, the way you put tricks across physically is vital. You need to appear confident, relaxed, in control and not remotely slippery.

1) Make as much eye contact with your audience as possible, as this will keep them looking at your face and not at your hands (see PRACTICE).

2) Look down at your hands as little as possible. By the time you do a trick in front of an audience it should be as much muscle memory as conscious action. Not

only will looking at your hands direct your audience's gaze that way but it means only your shoes will get the full benefit of your lovingly crafted patter.

3 ) Do it with flair. Nobody ever went to see a modest magician – or not willingly, at least – which is why so many give themselves names like The Great —, The Marvelous —, The Stupendous —, so make sure your performance has all the flourish and swagger it deserves. Put on a show.

4) Make tricks your own. There aren't too many new card tricks, indeed there haven't been for a very long time, but there are plenty of variations and room for a great deal more. So for every trick you learn, look for ways to customize it. That way, even if your audience has seen it before they won't have seen your version of it.

5) Concentrate on 'The Reveal'. A trick's reveal is the point at which you show your audience the mystery card or, er, reveal that you know what the card they picked is. And this is where your showmanship comes in, as it's this part of the trick that your audience will remember. Thus your reveals can be as flashy or as involved as you like, providing they are a) unexpected; and b) entertaining. In the course of *Card Tricks* there will be reveals that involve big drawings of cards pinned to your back and 'talking' cards, and I'll expect you to come up with reveals much more spectacular than those.

6) Less is more. Keep your performance to between 10 and 15 minutes or six tricks at the max. Anything over that and you risk repeating yourself or exceeding many people's natural concentration span.

# Seven Performance Pointers:

• Vary the types of tricks you do and never do two of the same kind together.

• Be aware that spectators will lie about what card they picked just to mess you up.

• Never, ever, tell them how a trick is done – remember, the audience wants to be amazed.

• Only ever do each trick once in each performance.

• Try not to let your audience get too close.

• Don't let the audience join in unless you've called for a volunteer – you're in charge here.

• If you get a trick wrong, end the performance there as you will have lost your audience's trust.

# Pick a Card ... any Card

What follows are some easy-to-master card trick techniques that will form the basis of all the tricks in *Card Tricks*. There is no out and out sleight of hand here, as that belongs in a more advanced setting, but there are enough card manipulation routines to point you in the direction of truly tricky hands.

(All descriptions are right-handed; left-handed people should simply substitute right for left.)

## The Glimpse

Sometimes called 'The Peek', this is going to become your very best friend as it is a selection of moves that will allow you to find out what the top or bottom card is on your deck. The Glimpse is the most vital part of any card magician's repertoire, as so many mind-reading, card moving or prediction tricks rely on you knowing what that card is. As the Glimpse is exactly what it says it is – a glimpse of the top or bottom card – some methods for achieving it will appear very obvious, but they still need to be practised in order to carry them off without arousing audience suspicion.

1) Straighten the cards by banging the edges on the table, but do so with the bottom card angled towards you.

2) During a riffle shuffle, bend the top card up enough to see what it is, and make sure it is the last card you let go (see SHUFFLING).

3) Blatantly look through the pack – this will need to be accompanied by some breezy, justifying patter – and remember the top card.

4) Give the deck to a spectator to shuffle and as it is given back tilt the bottom towards you – you'd be amazed at how regularly this happens naturally, as most

people don't think the bottom card matters therefore are frequently careless about displaying it.

5) Tilt the deck while doing an overhand shuffle, then make sure the bottom card stays there (see SHUFFLING).

The ideal top card Glimpse is to look at the bottom card and then bring it to the top while 'shuffling' (see RISE AND FALL).

## Shuffling – Genuinely or Otherwise

Genuine shuffles mix up the order of the cards, false shuffles keep them in exactly the same order, or, if this is what's required, keep the top or bottom card in place. The only two shuffles you'll need to know at this point are the Overhand Shuffle and the Riffling shuffle which, when used for their intended purpose, are carried out thus:

• The Overhand Shuffle (p.21) takes the deck sideways in the left hand while the right hand lifts a stack of them to drop back into the left hand in small random amounts on both sides of the accumulating pile.

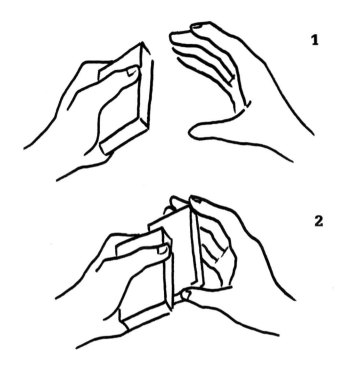

**1**

**2**

- The Riffling Shuffle (p.22) cuts the pack in half and places both halves face down on a table, practically touching each other. With your palms anchoring each stack, slightly raise the corners closest to each other with your thumbs and allow the cards to fall with each stack slotting into the other. Straighten into one stack.

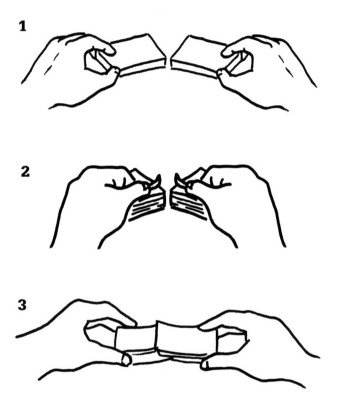

• Keeping the top or bottom card in place while shuffling can be very important, as it allows you to do the Glimpse (see p.18 and diagram below) and *then* appear to shuffle the pack; as most spectators will assume any trickery doesn't start until *after* the shuffle, it is far more likely your Glimpse will go undetected.

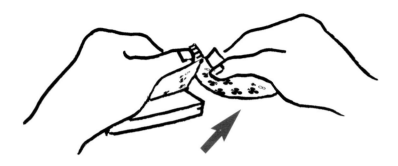

- To leave the top card in place with the Overhand Shuffle: with each shuffle, take the stack of cards from just behind the top card, while obscuring the top card with the hand that it is held in. Then make sure all 'random' dropping of cards goes on behind that top card. For the bottom card, take the stack from just above it and drop the cards behind it. With the Riffling Shuffle, after you have cut the deck and are performing the shuffle. make sure the original bottom card and/or the original top card are allowed to fall, respectively, before and after any other cards.

## Rise and Fall

For most tricks you will need to know the identity of the top card. It is much easier to glimpse the bottom card on a deck, so you'll need to know how to make it surreptitiously 'rise' to the top. Hold the pack as if for an Overhand Shuffle, keeping the back of your right hand in between your audience and the cards. Start to shuffle, bringing a stack of cards off the bottom and shuffling them on to the top. As you go on, shuffle the cards in smaller and smaller amounts until at the end you're doing it individually, merely still reversing their order as you put them on top of the deck. Hence the bottom card ends up on top.

Or, holding the cards facing into your left hand, hold back the bottom card with your left thumb. Then bring the remainder of the pack over the top of it effectively putting them underneath it and carry on your shuffling, making sure to only involve cards to the left of the top card.

If you want the top card to 'fall' to the bottom of the deck then reverse the pack in your hands so it is facing into your right hand and, once again using your left thumb, hold back the top card and bring the rest of the pack over it in exactly the same manner. This will put it on the bottom of the deck, so make sure the ensuing shuffle doesn't pick it up and that shuffled cards only land above it.

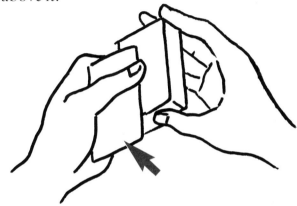

## The False Cut

To genuinely cut a deck of cards you simply cut it into two approximately equal stacks and put what was the bottom stack on to the top. However, to keep the original top card in place, hold it with the left thumb as the right hand, keeping in between the cards and the audience, pulls out the top half of the cards directly below that top card. As the top card falls back on to the top of the lower stack, the right hand puts the upper stack on the table, the left hand then comes across to put the lower stack, complete with prescribed top card, on top of it.

To keep the bottom card in place, the right hand holds the pack, slightly pinching the bottom card. The left hand then draws out the lower stack, leaving the bottom card behind, and places the lower stack on top of the upper stack.

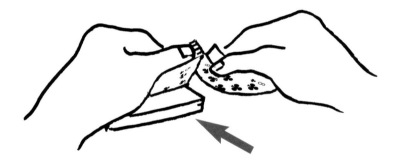

To avoid disturbing any of the order of the pack, a totally false cut is called for. This requires considerably more dexterity and confidence than the previous operations and should be practised hard before taking it to the stage. Hold the deck in your right hand, then using your index finger push the top stack into the left hand; keeping the left hand perfectly still, the right hand places its stack of cards on the table then moves up to take the cards from the left hand (which still mustn't move) and deposits them on top of the stack on the table. Nothing has changed.

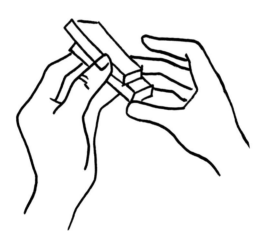

# And for my Next Trick ...

I bet you never thought we'd get to this point, but now you've done all the preparation and perfected all the sneaky moves. The card tricks listed below utilize one or more of the above techniques, and will simply mention the move rather than go over what it actually is. Although every trick is suitable for the absolute beginner, they have been arranged roughly in order of simplicity, with the most simple to get to grips with first. When the instructions call for you to invite a spectator to select a card, unless I've specified that they should show it to you assume this means they shouldn't. Although only a few of the explanations will instruct you to say stuff, take it as read that you should be treating your audience to your glossiest patter more or less all the time. Once again, it's important to remember that once you've mastered the tricks you should try to develop your own spin on them, which will make them unique. Give them a new name too, if you like.

Good luck.

## Good Vibrations

Probably the simplest of all card-finding tricks, this one uses techniques that will form the basis of several other tricks – glimpsing the bottom card and using it as a key card – and requires smooth but not over-elaborate patter. Thus it's as good a place as any to start.

Shuffle the deck and glimpse the bottom card – or, as with any trick that requires bottom card glimpsing, have an audience member shuffle it then carry out your glimpse as you take it back. Place the deck face down on the table and ask a spectator to cut it into two stacks. Have them look at the top card of what was the lower half, remember it and put it on top of what was the upper half. Then ask them to place the lower half on top of the other, apparently concealing the selected card deep in the deck but in fact placing the card you've glimpsed directly on top of it.

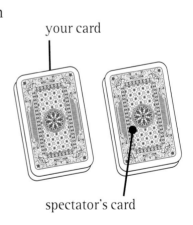

your card

spectator's card

Pick up the deck and start to deal the cards face up on the table. Don't do this too quickly and pay close attention to the cards, as the selected card will be the one dealt *after* the card you can identify. Remember what the selected card was, but carry on dealing the whole pack. Then, as theatrically as you like, start to get 'vibrations' from the pack, telling you what the selected card is and reveal it either by manually picking out, dealing back to it or simply naming it.

NB A variation of this trick is to proceed as above but to glimpse the top card of the deck, thus knowing the card that will be dealt *before* the selected card. While this means you can stop at the card concerned and don't have to deal past it, it rather precludes all the 'getting the vibrations from the pack' carry-on that is the making of this trick. As I'll keep reminding you, you're not a magic machine, you're there to entertain.

## Counting Off

One of the most straightforward card tricks known to man, this was the first trick I ever did and I taught it to

Canasta Jr when he was eight years old. In spite of it being very simple to execute, with personalization such as we employed it can be incredibly effective. Mrs Canasta is still trying to work out how it was done.

Counting Off is all about showmanship and how you present the very straightforward manoeuvre of an elementary card force. To force a card means to get your audience member to pick a particular card while, as far as they're concerned, they are choosing at random. In this case, it's the top card you are going to force and to perform this trick spectacularly you need to know what that top card is well in advance as you'll have a prop to prepare – the only one called for in *Card Tricks*. (It's worth remembering that tricks like this and Talk to the Queen, where you need to know the top or bottom card in advance as opposed from using the Glimpse, can be performed only as the first trick of your show.)

Holding the pack face down, shuffle to leave a card on top and ask your spectator to pick a number. From the top, deal that number of cards face down on to the table, counting off out loud. Pick up the pile you have just dealt and, still face down, deal them back on to the deck, once more counting out loud. 'Just checking', or something! Pick the top card off the deck and without looking at it show it to your spectator. Put it back low down the deck and shuffle to make sure it stays there.

Count off the same number of cards and hold up the last one – 'Is this your card?' It won't be, so act a little disappointed, shuffle (keeping the selected card near the bottom) and count off again. 'Is this your card?' It still won't be, so act rather upset and your audience will start to feel sorry for you – especially if this is your first trick. Shuffle and count off once more and

when the inevitable answer is 'No!', howl with anguish and turn your back in frustration. Have a large drawing of the card concerned pinned to your back. Other reveals can involve putting an identical card in the teapot or under the doormat or anywhere and telling your spectator to go and look for it, or, before you start the trick, giving another audience member an envelope with the name of the card sealed in it. But, personally, I prefer the mock failure approach as it gets a good laugh and immediately involves the audience. And it certainly went down a storm *Chez Canasta*.

## Under or Over

A very simple yet effective card force that involves what I like to call the Double Glimpse – you need to know both the top and bottom card in your deck.

Shuffle, leaving those two cards in place, then hand the deck to an audience member and ask them to cut it anywhere they like and place it on the table with what

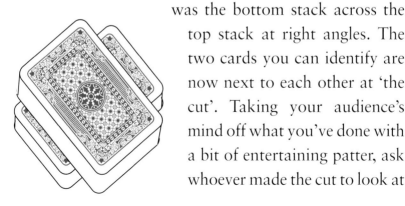

was the bottom stack across the top stack at right angles. The two cards you can identify are now next to each other at 'the cut'. Taking your audience's mind off what you've done with a bit of entertaining patter, ask whoever made the cut to look at either of the cards – make sure you remember which is which and which they picked up! – and then put the deck back together again. Shuffle and deal the cards face up until you come to theirs.

Of course, as one of the apprentices of Louis Canasta, I shall expect you to come up with a slightly more interesting reveal than that!

## Talk to the Queen

Another trick that involves knowing your bottom card in advance, and in this case it should be any queen. Shuffle the pack, keeping the queen in place, then cut the pack into four stacks placed face down on the table. Be aware of which stack came from the bottom of the deck.

Invite an audience member to pick a card from any stack, to look at it but not show it to you, and put it back. Now you put the deck back together by putting the bottom stack on top of the selected card, allowing you to identify it as it will be directly underneath your chosen queen, then put the other two stacks on top of that. If the spectator selects the top card of the bottom stack, ask them to cut that stack once before you rebuild the deck. That way your queen will still be on top of their card.

Cut the pack at approximately halfway, which will be well away from where the selected card is as that was on the top of the bottom of four roughly equal stacks, then spread the whole pack face up on the table.

Stare at them for a while and announce that one of the queens is trying to tell you something – this is where smooth patter and a slick performance is all that stands between you and ridicule! Pick up your chosen queen that is now *below* the spectator's card (you've inverted the pack) leaving an obvious gap where it was, hold it to your ear, pretend to be listening intently, nod and reach down for the card that was next to it, asking the queen if this is the card.

(You can ham this up a bit by first reaching for the card on the other side of where the queen was and pretending you misheard her the choice is yours.)

## Have You Seen It Yet?

A Counting Cards trick that relies on your ability to count off 21 cards in the deck quickly and unnoticed as you sort through the deck. This isn't as hard as you might imagine – hold the cards face down and push them over from your right to your left hand and practise counting them off in four groups of five plus one, as it's far easier to keep track surreptitiously of smaller groups of cards.

Fan a deck of cards out face down and invite an audience member to take one. Restack the deck into your right hand, start spreading the cards into your left hand, apparently at random, but when you've counted 21 across ask them to return their card to the deck as the 22nd card. Restack the deck and begin dealing the cards into two stacks on the table, one face up and one face down, starting with a face-up card – it is vital that you start the deal with the face-up stack. Chat to your audience and ask whoever picked the card to stop you when you get to it. When you've dealt all the cards, ask 'Have you seen it yet?', to which the answer will be 'No.'

Pick up the face-down pile and deal them in exactly the same way – starting with a face-up pile – and at the end once again ask, 'Have you seen it yet?', to which you'll get the same response. Carry on like this, taking and dealing out smaller and smaller face-down stacks and asking the same question until you have one face-down card left – that will be the card your spectator picked.

## The Clock Never Lies

Another Counting Cards trick, only this time you'll need to be able to count off 13 cards – the best way to do that is three lots of four and a one.

Shuffle the deck, then count off 13 cards without your audience realizing what you're doing. Hand this apparently random stack to a spectator and place the remainder of the deck face down on the table. Ask them to count off some cards from this stack and put them in their pocket, then to look at and remember the bottom card of what they've got left in their hands, and to put them face down on top of the stack on the table. You will have your back turned while they do this, so you obviously cannot observe any part of the proceedings.

After you have been invited to turn back, deal the cards out *anti-clockwise and starting at 12 o'clock* to represent a clockface with 12 cards arranged as the digits and the remainder stacked in the middle. It is vital you remember to deal anti-clockwise. Ask the spectator to remove the cards from their pocket, to count them and tell them the card they selected should be at that 'o'clock' on the clockface. Have them deal their cards on to the clockface *clockwise and starting at one o'clock*, counting as they go – 'One o'clock … two o'clock …' and so on. Then get them to pick up both cards at the last clockface digit they dealt, turn them over and the bottom card will be theirs.

12 o'clock position

remainder of pack

3 o'clock position

## Copping Off

In which two cards, apparently inserted into a deck at very different places, are so keen to become an item that they end up snuggled down next to each other. This is due entirely to the power of their lurrrve and with no obvious help from a third party.

Pass the deck to an audience member and ask them to shuffle it and cut it into two roughly equal stacks, giving one to you and keeping the other themselves. At this point, you will glimpse the bottom card of your stack. Ask your spectator to select a card from their stack, not to show it to you but look at it, remember it and put it back on top of the stack, while you make a show of doing the same. The big difference, though, is that you really don't need to remember your card as it doesn't matter at all – the important card here is the one on the bottom of your stack.

The spectator puts his stack face down on the table, and you put yours on top of it. The two selected cards are now separated by half of the deck, but the card you glimpsed, previously the bottom of your stack, is now on top of your spectator's card. Explain that the two selected cards fancy each other and they will come together despite being kept apart – feel free to make as many Romeo and Juliet references as you like. Ask the spectator what their card was, name the card you glimpsed, stroke rather than bang the deck – hey, this is a lurrrve thang – spread it face up and the two named cards will be nestled next to each other in the centre.

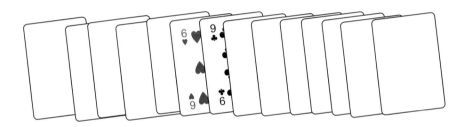

## The Piano Player

This trick is all about the power of suggestion – you will be manipulating your audience rather than the cards, so you'll need to be slick, confident and very swish with the patter.

Make a big show of selecting an audience member

with 'piano player's hands' – however you choose to define this is entirely up to you – and have them sit at the table with their hands arranged on it as if their fingers were arched over a keyboard. Shuffle and select, completely at random, fifteen cards from the deck. What the cards are really doesn't matter for this trick as all you need is the right number. Place the cards in pairs between your spectator's fingers, with a single card between the last one.

**1**

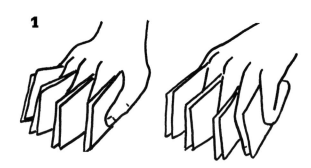

Once this is done, take the first pair and place them on the table face down and next to each other; take the next pair and place each one face down on one of the other cards; continue until you have built up two small stacks with one odd card over.

**2**

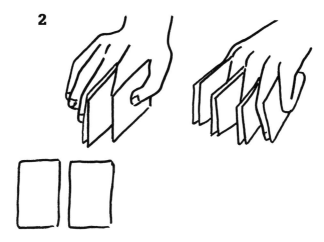

Ask your audience which stack you should put this odd card on – make sure you perpetually refer to it as the 'odd card' – and follow their directions.

Inform them that you can make the odd card jump from one stack to another and pick up the stack with the odd card on. Weave your magic, and deal the cards in pairs into a single pile. There will be no odd card left over. Then pick up the other stack and deal that out in pairs and you will be left holding a single, odd card.

To figure out how this trick works, divide your original 15 cards by two and you'll realize that the original stacks only ever had seven cards in them and the 'odd' card in fact made the chosen stack an even number. It's down to your clever presentation to make sure your audience doesn't get the chance to figure it out too.

## The Sandwich

This is trick that needs help from three audience members, as each has to select a card to become the bread and the meat for the sandwich. It also requires skilful manipulation of the pack to cut it in precisely the right place.

Shuffle the deck and ask two audience members to pick a card each, remember them and ask them to put both back on top of the deck. Glimpse the bottom card, cut the deck and put what was the bottom half on top so you know the card that is on top of the two chosen cards. Explain that your two volunteers have chosen the bread for the sandwich, now you need somebody to select the meat to go in between. Spread the deck on the table face up and invite *another* spectator to remove a card other than the two already selected – after all, they're bread so they can't be meat as well.

You will be able to see the two previously selected cards as they'll be on top of the card you glimpsed, so when you gather up the deck to turn it over and cut it, you can slide the tip of your little finger in between the two chosen cards and cut the deck there. Now, when you put the deck back together after the cut one slice of bread will be at the bottom and the other at the top.

Invite the spectator who is holding the meat, so to speak, to place it on top of the deck and cut it so the bottom card comes up to sit on top of it. Ask the first two spectators what their cards were and spread the deck face up to reveal the sandwich has been made and their cards are on either side of the third card selected.

## You Do It, Then!

For this trick you will need to be a reasonably skilled card handler, as you'll have to use your little finger to mark a card that you need to bring to the top. This is also one of the very rare occasions when you'll allow an audience member do a bit of magic – but don't worry, you'll stay in complete control and apparently be 'channelling' your powers into them! For this reason, provided you can make a big enough show of transferring your powers and maybe having them grow weak, You Do It, Then! is a good trick to finish on.

Shuffle a deck, fan it out face down and invite a member of the audience to remove a card and look at it.

 As soon as they remove the card, reform the deck and start a slow, casual overhand shuffle. Have the spectator replace the card in the deck as you shuffle, but mark it by inserting the tip of your little finger on top of it and continue shuffling to bring it to the top.

## And for my Next Trick ...

Ask the spectator to think of a number between 1 and 10, and deal that many cards face down on to the table. With a theatrical flourish, turn over the top card of this stack, announcing it to be the selected card. It isn't, it's on the bottom of that stack because you brought it up to the top of the deck. Attempting to mask your disappointment, go into an explanation about weakening powers and ask for somebody to help you. Make a show of transferring what's left of your powers to them – laying on of hands ... chanting ... anything! – have them turn the top card back face down, pick up the stack and re-deal it, face down, turning over the last card. Of course, this one is the selected card.

# Useful Websites

http://ecardtricks.com

http://magic.about.com/library/tricks/
bltrickmenucards.htm

http://web.superb.net/cardtric

http://www.cardtricks.org